KU-687-798

contents

foreword

Bridge is a game enjoyed by many millions of players all over the world.

In these days of rising commercial pressures, increasing leisure and greater longevity, bridge has the potential to break down social and ethnic barriers and to keep the wheels of the brain turning in both the old and the young. Apart from that, bridge at whatever level is a very inexpensive game, all you need to play is a flat surface that the four players can sit round with a pack of cards and, of course, an understanding as to how to play the game.

It is for these reasons that I am particularly pleased to welcome the 'How to Play Bridge' series which has been specially designed to make the game easy to follow for beginners, no matter what their age. I believe that you will find the whole series well presented and particularly easy to read.

Bobby Wolff
Dallas, Texas
March 1997

PLAYING
with
TRUMPS

SALLY BROCK
Foreword by BOBBY WOLFF

HOW TO PLAY BRIDGE

BT BATSFORD LTD, LONDON

First published 1998
© Sally Brock 1998

ISBN 0 7134 8252 4

Typeset by Apsbridge Services Ltd, Nottingham
Printed in Singapore
for the publishers,
B. T. Batsford Ltd, 583 Fulham Road,
London SW6 5BY

A BATSFORD BRIDGE BOOK
Series editor: Tony Sowter

introduction

Sometimes play in a suit contract is exactly the same as in no trumps. Perhaps the bidding has been less than accurate and no trumps would have been a better contract. All that declarer must do is draw trumps and establish winners using the various techniques that are discussed more fully in the companion book in this series *No Trump Play.*

On other occasions the trump suit really comes into its element and makes a significant difference. There are various techniques that must be learned: trumping (usually called ruffing) losers, cross-ruffing, suit establishment, the ruffing finesse, elimination plays and so on. However, perhaps the most important thing to learn is *when* to apply these techniques. Inexperienced players find it very difficult to know when to draw trumps: sometimes they draw trumps when they should be taking ruffs in the dummy, while on other occasions they fail to draw trumps only to find that one of their winners is ruffed.

This book contains thirty separate deals, each of which takes three pages. On the first page a full deal is presented, along with the bidding and opening lead. A line of play is described that failed to make the contract. You, the reader, are asked 'Can you do better?' You should pause here and think about what 'declarer' (i.e. the person playing the hand) has done and see if you can spot his error.

On the subsequent two pages it is pointed out where declarer went wrong and what he should have done. Then the play is described trick by trick. The easiest way to follow this is to get a pack of cards, deal out the hand and play it through, card by card. You can do this on your own or with friends. You should then be able to see the positions that develop. Other than actually playing bridge for ten years or so, this is the best way I know of improving your bridge play.

At the end of each deal, the main lesson to be learned is highlighted for easy reference.

Whatever else, I am sure you will be a better player by the time you finish the thirty deals than you were when you started.

deal 1

no trump play in a suit contract

The first hand is very easy, to get you off to a good start.

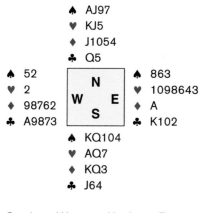

```
              ♠  AJ97
              ♥  KJ5
              ♦  J1054
              ♣  Q5
  ♠  52                      ♠  863
  ♥  2          N           ♥  1098643
  ♦  98762   W     E        ♦  A
  ♣  A9873      S           ♣  K102
              ♠  KQ104
              ♥  AQ7
              ♦  KQ3
              ♣  J64
```

South	West	North	East
1NT	Pass	2♣	Pass
2♠	Pass	4♠	All Pass

West led the two of hearts against four spades. Declarer won with the ace and played a club to dummy's queen and East's king. East cashed the ace of diamonds and played a second heart. The defenders now cross-ruffed four tricks and West made his ace of clubs. Four down. Can you do better?

What went wrong?

Declarer failed to count his winners and losers. There are ten tricks on top: four spades, three hearts and three diamonds (once the ace has been knocked out).

What should declarer have done?

He should simply have drawn trumps and then played on diamonds.

The play

Trick 1: Win the ace of hearts.

Trick 2: Cash the king of spades.

Trick 3: Play a spade to dummy's ace.

Trick 4: Play a third spade to your queen. In this instance you have now drawn all East/West's trumps but if an opponent still had a trump left you should play an extra round.

Trick 5: Play the king of diamonds to East's ace.

Tricks 6-13: Win East's heart return, cash your three diamonds and your other top heart, making ten tricks in all.

Note that West could have beaten you by leading a diamond at trick one. He chose not to do that – make him pay!

If you have
sufficient
winners and there is
no danger of the
opponents cashing too many
tricks when they get the lead, draw
trumps as quickly as you can.

deal 2
a wide open suit

```
              ♠ AJ97
              ♥ KJ5
              ♦ J1054
              ♣ Q5
♠ 8652                        ♠ 3
♥ 32          N               ♥ 109864
♦ 862       W   E             ♦ A97
♣ AJ83        S               ♣ K1092
              ♠ KQ104
              ♥ AQ7
              ♦ KQ3
              ♣ 764
```

South	West	North	East
1NT	Pass	2♣	Pass
2♠	Pass	4♠	All Pass

West led the three of hearts against four spades.
This time declarer won the lead, drew trumps in
four rounds and played a diamond towards his
hand. But East went in with the ace and
switched to a club. The defenders took four
club tricks and declarer went two
down. Can you do better?

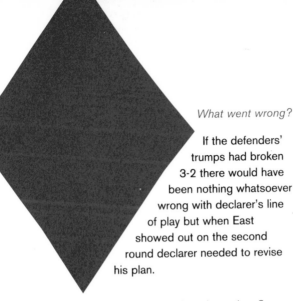

If the defenders' trumps had broken 3-2 there would have been nothing whatsoever wrong with declarer's line of play but when East showed out on the second round declarer needed to revise his plan.

What should declarer have done?

Drawing three rounds of trumps is fine but then declarer must play a diamond while he still has a trump left in each hand. The best East can do is duck a couple of diamonds but when the suit breaks 3-3 declarer is home. When East wins the ace of diamonds and plays clubs, declarer ruffs the third round in dummy, plays a heart to his hand and draws the last trump.

The play

Trick 1: Win the queen of hearts.

Tricks 2-4: Play three rounds of trumps, East showing out on the second.

Tricks 5-7: Play diamonds, East winning the third round.

Tricks 8-10: The defenders play three rounds of clubs, the third of which you ruff in the dummy.

Trick 11: Play a heart to your ace.
Trick 12: Cash the ten of spades, drawing West's last trump.
Trick 13: Cash your last heart – ten tricks in all.

If you have a wide open suit, you may not be able to draw all the trumps until you have finished establishing your side winners.

deal 3
take that discard

```
            ♠ 109843
            ♥ QJ32
            ♦ Q2
            ♣ A3
♠ A7          ┌─────────┐      ♠ K
♥ 10974       │    N    │      ♥ AK65
♦ 976       W │         │ E    ♦ J10843
♣ KQ102       │    S    │      ♣ 985
              └─────────┘
            ♠ QJ652
            ♥ 8
            ♦ AK5
            ♣ J764
```

South	West	North	East
South	*West*	*North*	*East*
1♠	Pass	4♠	All Pass

West led the king of clubs against four
spades. Declarer won the ace and played
a trump. East won his king, cashed the
king of hearts and played a second
club. West won his queen and still
had the ace of trumps to come,
so that was one down. Can
you do better?

What went wrong?

Declarer had counted his winners all right: three trumps in each hand by ruffing after the ace and king had been knocked out, three diamonds and one club, making ten in total. What he failed to do was count his losers: two spades, one heart and a club that was set up by the opening lead.

What should declarer have done?

He should have played three rounds of diamonds, discarding dummy's club loser *before* touching trumps.

The play

Trick 1: Win the ace of clubs.
Tricks 2-4: Play the queen of diamonds and then the ace and king of diamonds, discarding a club from dummy.

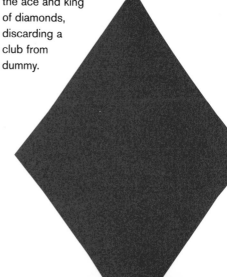

Trick 5: Play a spade which loses to East's king.

Trick 6: East returns a club which you ruff in dummy.

Trick 7: Play a heart. East wins with the king.

Trick 8: East returns another club which again you ruff in dummy.

Tricks 9-13: A heart ruff in hand and a club ruff in dummy leaves you with just trumps left in hand. West can make his ace whenever he feels like it but that will be all.

Don't forget to count your losers as well as your winners.

deal 4
a ruff in dummy

```
              ♠ 76
              ♥ KQ4
              ♦ J652
              ♣ Q742
  ♠ 109842    ┌─────────┐    ♠ QJ5
  ♥ 2         │    N    │    ♥ 653
  ♦ K104      │ W     E │    ♦ Q97
  ♣ J1095     │    S    │    ♣ AK83
              └─────────┘
              ♠ AK3
              ♥ AJ10987
              ♦ A83
              ♣ 6
```

South	West	North	East
1♥	Pass	2♥	Pass
4♥	All Pass		

West led the jack of clubs against four hearts. Declarer played low from dummy to the first trick and West continued at trick two with a second club. Declarer ruffed in hand and drew trumps. He then tried ducking a diamond but the defence was accurate and he was quickly one down. Can you do better?

What went wrong?

Declarer failed to count his tricks. He has two spades, six hearts and one diamond, nine in all. His best bet for a tenth trick is to ruff a spade in the dummy.

What should declarer have done?

He should have ruffed the second club and drawn *two* rounds of trumps only, with the ace and king. He then cashes the ace and king of spades and ruffs a spade with the queen of hearts. Finally, he comes to hand with a club ruff to finish drawing trumps and cash his winners.

The play

Trick 1: West's jack of clubs wins.
Trick 2: Ruff East's king of clubs.
Tricks 3-4: Play the ace and king of hearts.
Tricks 5-6: Cash the ace and king of spades.
Trick 7: Play the three of spades and ruff with dummy's queen of hearts. On this occasion it is extremely unlikely that East is also out of spades (that would leave West with a six-card suit and he would probably have bid over your one heart opening). Nevertheless, why take chances? It was easy enough to leave a high trump in dummy to make sure that you would not be overruffed.

Trick 8: Ruff a club to get back to hand.

Trick 9: Draw East's last trump.

Tricks 10-13: Cash your heart winners and your ace of diamonds – ten tricks in all.

If you have a singleton or doubleton in the same hand as your shorter trumps, you may need to take a ruff in that hand before drawing all the trumps.

deal 5
two ruffs in dummy

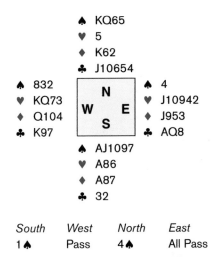

```
              ♠ KQ65
              ♥ 5
              ♦ K62
              ♣ J10654
  ♠ 832          N        ♠ 4
  ♥ KQ73       W   E      ♥ J10942
  ♦ Q104         S        ♦ J953
  ♣ K97                   ♣ AQ8
              ♠ AJ1097
              ♥ A86
              ♦ A87
              ♣ 32
```

South	*West*	*North*	*East*
1♠	Pass	4♠	All Pass

West led the king of hearts against four spades.
Declarer won the ace and drew three rounds of
trumps. He then played a club. East won and
continued with a second heart which declarer
ruffed in dummy. Declarer played a second club.
This time West won his king. He cashed the queen
of hearts and played a fourth heart which declarer
ruffed. Declarer played a diamond to dummy's king
and ruffed a club. This established two winners in
dummy but there was no way to reach them. Can
you do better?

Once again declarer failed to count his tricks. He has five spades, one heart and two diamonds. He needs to find two more tricks. The easiest way to make them is to ruff *two* hearts in dummy.

What should declarer have done?

He should have won the opening lead and ruffed a heart. He then plays a spade to his hand, ruffs a second heart, draws trumps and claims his contract.

The play

Trick 1: Win the ace of hearts.
Trick 2: Ruff a heart with the king of spades.
Trick 3: Play the five of spades to your nine.
Trick 4: Ruff a heart with the queen of spades.

Trick 5: Play the six of spades to your ten.

Trick 6: Cash the ace of spades, drawing West's last trump.

Tricks 7-10: Cash your remaining trump and diamond winners, making ten tricks in all.

If you count
your winners and
losers on every hand
you should be able to work
out when you can afford to draw
the trumps.

deal 6
no ruffing needed

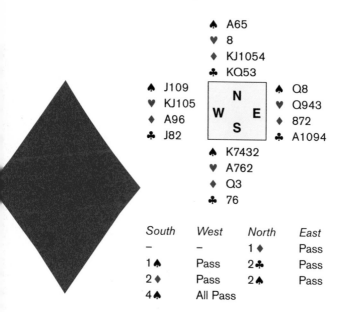

```
                    ♠ A65
                    ♥ 8
                    ♦ KJ1054
                    ♣ KQ53
        ♠ J109          N          ♠ Q8
        ♥ KJ105     W       E      ♥ Q943
        ♦ A96           S          ♦ 872
        ♣ J82                      ♣ A1094
                    ♠ K7432
                    ♥ A762
                    ♦ Q3
                    ♣ 76
```

South	West	North	East
–	–	1♦	Pass
1♠	Pass	2♣	Pass
2♦	Pass	2♠	Pass
4♠	All Pass		

West led the jack of trumps against four spades.
Declarer won the ace, played a heart to the ace
and ruffed a heart. He then played a diamond to his
queen. West defended well by refusing to win this
trick. Declarer ruffed a second heart and played the
king of diamonds. This time West won and cashed
a heart. He had to come to a trump and a club at
the end. Can you do better?

What went wrong?

Declarer should have seen that he didn't have enough trumps to ruff all his hearts. That should have been enough to persuade him to look for a different line – playing on diamonds, for example.

What should he have done?

He should have won the trump lead in hand and played the queen of diamonds immediately. West does best to win the second diamond but he has no good defence. Suppose he plays a heart. Declarer wins the ace, plays a trump to dummy's ace and plays out his diamonds, discarding hearts from hand. West can ruff whenever he likes but it will do him no good. Declarer loses only a trump and the two minor-suit aces.

The play

Trick 1:   Win the king of spades.

Trick 2:   Play the queen of diamonds, ducked by West.

Trick 3:   Play another diamond to West's ace.

Trick 4:   West switches to a heart. You win with the ace.

Trick 5:   Play a trump to dummy's ace.

Tricks 6-7:   Cash the king and jack of diamonds, discarding hearts. West ruffs the second top diamond.

Tricks 8-9:   West plays a club to his partner's ace and East plays a second club which you win in dummy.

Tricks 10-13:   You can now claim the rest. Discard your last heart on your fifth diamond and all you have left is trumps. Ten tricks in all.

Just because you have a singleton in the dummy along with a few trumps doesn't necessarily mean that the right play is to take ruffs in the dummy.

deal 7
keeping communications open

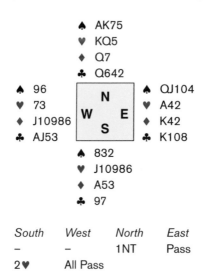

```
              ♠ AK75
              ♥ KQ5
              ♦ Q7
              ♣ Q642
    ♠ 96                    ♠ QJ104
    ♥ 73          N         ♥ A42
    ♦ J10986    W   E       ♦ K42
    ♣ AJ53        S         ♣ K108
              ♠ 832
              ♥ J10986
              ♦ A53
              ♣ 97
```

South	West	North	East
–	–	1NT	Pass
2♥	All Pass		

West led the jack of diamonds against two
hearts. Declarer tried dummy's queen and won
East's king with his ace. He then played a
second diamond. West won and played a
trump. Declarer played the king of
trumps from dummy but East did well –
he ducked. Declarer took his best
chance by playing ace, king and another
spade but the suit did not break. East
played ace and another heart and declarer
had to go one down. Can you do better?

25 ♣

What went wrong?

Declarer was not guilty of failing to count his tricks this time. He knew he needed to ruff a diamond in the dummy. But he failed to appreciate his communication problems.

What should declarer have done?

He should simply duck East's king of diamonds at trick one. Suppose East switches to a low trump. Declarer can win in either hand, cash the ace of diamonds and ruff a diamond before playing a second trump.

The play

Trick 1: East's king of diamonds wins the first trick.

Trick 2: East switches to a trump which runs round to dummy's king.

Trick 3: Play a diamond to your ace.

Trick 4: Ruff your five of diamonds with dummy's queen of hearts.

Trick 5: Play a trump. East wins with the ace.

Trick 6: East plays the queen of spades which you win in dummy with the king.

Trick 7: Cash the ace of spades.

Trick 8: Play a third spade. East wins while West discards a diamond.

Trick 9: East plays a fourth spade which you ruff.

Tricks 10-11: You cash two more trump tricks, bringing your total to eight.

When you have the ace with two or three small cards facing a small doubleton, it often makes communications easier if you duck the first round of the suit.

deal 8
cross-ruff

```
                    ♠ QJ1092
                    ♥ 5
                    ♦ 109762
                    ♣ 85
    ♠ 64                           ♠ 5
    ♥ K10          ┌─────────┐     ♥ QJ984
    ♦ AQ3          │    N    │     ♦ KJ854
    ♣ AQ10943      │ W     E │     ♣ K2
                   │    S    │
                   └─────────┘
                    ♠ AK873
                    ♥ A7632
                    ♦ –
                    ♣ J76
```

South	West	North	East
–	1♣	Pass	1♥
1♠	2♣	4♠	All Pass

West led the four of trumps against four
spades. Declarer won the lead and drew a
second round of trumps. He then cashed
the ace of hearts and ruffed hearts in
dummy and diamonds in hand. As
play progressed it slowed down
somewhat as he realised that he
was going to end up with only nine
tricks. Can you do better?

What went wrong?

Declarer can count one top spade (trick one), four more spade tricks by ruffing in each hand (making eight more in total) and the ace of hearts – ten certain tricks.

What should he have done?

He should not have drawn a second round of trumps.

The play

Trick 1: Win trick one with the seven of spades.

Trick 2: Cash the ace of hearts. Note that you cannot afford to draw a second round of trumps. If you do you can make only eight trump tricks in total, one less than you need.

Trick 3: Ruff a heart in the dummy.

Trick 4: Ruff a diamond in your hand.

Trick 5: Ruff a second heart in the dummy.

Trick 6: Ruff a second diamond in your hand.

Trick 7: Ruff a third heart in the dummy.

Trick 8: Ruff a third diamond in your hand.

Trick 9: Ruff your last heart in dummy.

Trick 10: Ruff a fourth diamond in hand with your last trump. You have made the first ten tricks.

Tricks 11-13: You have no further interest in taking any tricks!

When planning a cross-ruff you not only need sufficient trumps, you also need sufficient cards to ruff. Here you had plenty of losers to ruff in both hearts and diamonds.

When you have a good fit with long trumps in both hands and shortage facing length in the side suits, consider trying to play a complete cross-ruff.

deal 9
suit establishment

```
              ♠ Q7
              ♥ AK3
              ♦ AK984
              ♣ J82
  ♠ AK53                   ♠ J10982
  ♥ 52         N           ♥ 96
  ♦ J632    W     E        ♦ Q10
  ♣ Q93        S           ♣ K1054
              ♠ 64
              ♥ QJ10874
              ♦ 75
              ♣ A76
```

South	West	North	East
–	–	1NT	Pass
4♥	All Pass		

West led the ace and king of spades against
four hearts and then switched to the three of
clubs. Declarer won the ace of clubs and
drew trumps. He now cashed the ace
and king of diamonds and ruffed a
diamond. He crossed back to
dummy with a trump and ruffed a
second diamond but then had no
entry back to the established nine so
had to go one down. Can you do better?

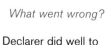

What went wrong?

Declarer did well to recognise that he needed to set up the diamond suit, but he failed to appreciate his entry problems.

What should declarer have done?

He should have won the club switch in hand, played the queen of trumps from hand and then played diamonds – ace, king and a third diamond, ruffing with a high trump. Now a trump to dummy and another diamond ruff. He can then cross to dummy with a third trump to cash his established diamond trick.

The play

Tricks 1-2: West cashes his top spades.
Trick 3: Win the ace of clubs.
Trick 4: Cash the queen of hearts. Always draw as many trumps as you can afford before playing on a side suit.
Tricks 5-6: Cash the ace and king of diamonds.
Trick 7: Ruff a diamond with the jack of trumps.
Trick 8: Play a trump to dummy's king.
Trick 9: Ruff a diamond with the ten of trumps.

Trick 10: Cross back to dummy with the ace
of hearts. On this occasion all the
trumps have already gone, but if not
this would draw the last one.

Trick 11: Cash dummy's nine of diamonds.

Trick 12: You still have a trump left for your
tenth trick.

When
dummy has a
long suit, think about
trying to establish length
tricks in it – but remember
to watch your entries.

deal 10
catering for bad breaks

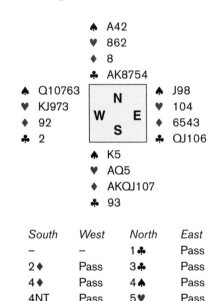

	♠	A42
	♥	862
	♦	8
	♣	AK8754

♠	Q10763		♠	J98
♥	KJ973		♥	104
♦	92		♦	6543
♣	2		♣	QJ106

	♠	K5
	♥	AQ5
	♦	AKQJ107
	♣	93

South	West	North	East
–	–	1♣	Pass
2♦	Pass	3♣	Pass
4♦	Pass	4♠	Pass
4NT	Pass	5♥	Pass
6♦	All Pass		

West led the two of trumps against six diamonds.
Declarer drew trumps, cashed the ace and king of
clubs and ruffed a club. He now crossed to the ace
of spades but his club suit was not established so
he fell back on the heart finesse. When it was
wrong he had to go down. Can you do better?

What went wrong?

Declarer did not keep his eye on the number of tricks he was trying to make. His line would have been perfect if he had been trying to make all thirteen tricks but that was not the contract.

What should declarer have done?

After drawing trumps, he should have ducked a club altogether! East wins the ten and continues, say, with a heart. Declarer rises with the ace, cashes the ace and king of clubs, discarding a heart, and ruffs a club. He now crosses to dummy's ace of spades and has two good clubs on which to discard his heart loser.

The play

Trick 1:	Win the two of diamonds with the ten.
Tricks 2-4:	Draw three more rounds of trumps, discarding a spade and two hearts from the dummy.
Trick 5:	Play the nine of clubs from hand and a small club from dummy whatever West plays.
Trick 6:	Win the heart return with the ace.
Trick 7:	Play a club to the king.
Trick 8:	Cash the ace of clubs.

Trick 9: Ruff a club, establishing the suit.

Trick 10: Cross to dummy's ace of spades.

Trick 11: Discard your last heart loser on one of dummy's club winners.

Tricks 12-13: Claim the last two tricks with your master trump and your king of spades.

Ducking
one round
can often help
to establish a
side suit.

deal 11
the ruffing finesse

```
              ♠ –
              ♥ AK984
              ♦ A752
              ♣ J743
♠ A97652       ┌─────────┐       ♠ 843
♥ 72           │    N    │       ♥ 3
♦ 104        W │         │ E     ♦ KQJ963
♣ Q82          │    S    │       ♣ K95
               └─────────┘
              ♠ KQJ10
              ♥ QJ1065
              ♦ 8
              ♣ A106
```

South	West	North	East
South	*West*	*North*	*East*
1♥	Pass	6♥	All Pass

North had a difficult bid to find over his partner's
opening bid, especially with no specialist
convention to help him. He showed good
judgement of his general strength with
his direct pot at slam.

West led the ten of diamonds. Declarer
won the ace and drew trumps. He now
played on cross-ruff lines, alternately ruffing
diamonds and spades. Finally he played a club
but West won and cashed the ace of spades.
One down. Can you do better?

Declarer had plenty of tricks: three spades (after he had lost the ace), five trumps in hand and three ruffs in dummy, the ace of diamonds and the ace of clubs – thirteen in all. All he had to do was be prepared to lose a trick – to the ace of spades.

What should declarer have done?

He should have drawn trumps ending in hand and played the king of spades, running it if West played low. This playing of a top honor from a sequence when there is a void in the dummy, intending to run it if it is not covered, is known as a 'ruffing finesse'.

The play

Trick 1: Win the ace of diamonds.
Tricks 2-3: Draw two rounds of trumps ending in hand.
Trick 4: Play the king of spades. West will probably duck this time and you throw a club from dummy.

Trick 5: Play the queen of spades. West covers and you ruff in dummy.

Trick 6: Ruff a diamond back to hand.

Tricks 7-8: Cash your two established spades discarding clubs from dummy.

Tricks 9-13: Cash the ace of clubs and cross-ruff the last four tricks, making an overtrick. If East had had the ace of spades instead of West you would have made only twelve tricks.

A ruffing finesse is a little like knocking out winners in a no trump contract, except that sometimes you don't have to lose a trick!

deal 12
a double ruffing finesse

```
              ♠ KQ8
              ♥ 64
              ♦ QJ10983
              ♣ 54
   ♠ -                       ♠ 543
   ♥ KJ3          N          ♥ Q1097
   ♦ A76      W       E      ♦ K542
   ♣ KQJ10863     S          ♣ 92
              ♠ AJ109762
              ♥ A852
              ♦ -
              ♣ A7
```

South	West	North	East
1♠	Double	2♠	Pass
3♥	4♣	4♠	Pass
6♠	All Pass		

West led the king of clubs against six spades. Declarer couldn't see any way to make his contract. He played ace and another heart. West won the jack, cashed the queen of clubs and then tried to cash the ace of diamonds. Declarer ruffed and was able to ruff two hearts in the dummy to end up only one down. Can you do better?

This is quite a difficult hand and it is easy to understand why declarer couldn't see a way to give himself a chance. The last hand featured a ruffing finesse. This hand takes that idea a stage further.

What should declarer have done?

Look at that diamond suit. Suppose declarer leads the queen from dummy. East plays low, declarer discards a club and West wins his ace. Later on declarer crosses back to dummy and plays the jack of diamonds. East has no winning play. If he covers declarer ruffs and crosses back to dummy to cash the suit; if he doesn't cover declarer discards and then plays the ten of diamonds... The only problem may be entries: two entries are needed to establish the suit and one more to get back to cash it. On this hand he is lucky as he has three trump entries.

The play

Trick 1: Win the ace of clubs.
Trick 2: Play a spade to dummy's queen. On this occasion West shows out – not much of a surprise given his enthusiastic bidding.
Trick 3: Play the queen of diamonds. When East plays low, you discard a club and West wins his ace.
Trick 4: West tries to cash his queen of clubs but you ruff.

Trick 5: Play the seven of spades to dummy's eight.

Trick 6: Play the jack of diamonds from dummy. East plays low and you discard a heart.

Trick 7: Play the ten of diamonds. This time East covers and you ruff.

Trick 8: Play the ten of spades to dummy's jack, drawing East's last trump.

Tricks 9-13: Cash two more diamonds discarding your remaining heart losers and claim the remainder with your high trumps and the ace of hearts.

For this play to succeed you just needed East to have one of the ace or king of diamonds. This is very likely (about 75%) in any event, but in this particular instance it is almost 100% because West would surely have led a diamond at trick one had he held both the ace and king.

When you have a long good suit facing a void the best way to establish it may be to take one or more ruffing finesses.

deal 13
simple avoidance play

```
           ♠ K1097
           ♥ A3
           ♦ 86
           ♣ K10532
♠ 83                      ♠ 62
♥ KQ1052      N           ♥ J94
♦ A1094    W     E        ♦ QJ732
♣ 98          S           ♣ Q76
           ♠ AQJ54
           ♥ 876
           ♦ K5
           ♣ AJ4
```

South	West	North	East
1♠	Pass	3♠	Pass
4♠	All Pass		

West led the king of hearts against four
spades. Declarer won with the ace,
drew trumps and played the ace
of clubs and jack of clubs,
running it to East's queen.
East switched to the queen
of diamonds and declarer
finished one down, the
defenders taking one heart,
two diamonds and a club.
Can you do better?

What went wrong?

Declarer should have appreciated that East was the danger hand. Only if he gained the lead to play a diamond through the king was the contract in jeopardy.

What should declarer have done?

He should have ducked the heart lead to start with, otherwise West could later put his partner in with the jack. He should win the continuation, draw trumps ending in the dummy and play a club to the jack. This time he would be rewarded with two overtricks for his efforts.

The play

Trick 1: Duck the king of hearts.

Trick 2: Win the heart continuation in dummy.

Tricks 3-4: Draw trumps ending in dummy. On this occasion you only need to play two rounds but there is no danger in playing a third round if you have to.

Trick 5: Play a club to your jack. On this occasion the jack wins. However, should the jack lose because the queen is with West the diamonds are safe from attack. Ten tricks are unstoppable.

Trick 6: Cash the ace of clubs.

Trick 7: Play a club to dummy's king.

Tricks 8-9: Cash your other club winners discarding diamonds from hand.

Tricks 10-13: Cross-ruff the remaining four tricks.

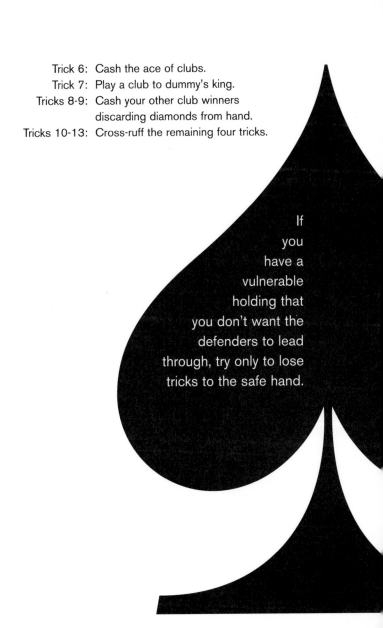

If you have a vulnerable holding that you don't want the defenders to lead through, try only to lose tricks to the safe hand.

deal 14
finesse or ruffing finesse?

```
              ♠ AQJ10
              ♥ K53
              ♦ J107
              ♣ K83
  ♠ K8542                    ♠ 976
  ♥ 86         N             ♥ QJ1042
  ♦ 8432    W     E          ♦ 6
  ♣ 76         S             ♣ AJ109
              ♠ 3
              ♥ A97
              ♦ AKQ95
              ♣ Q542
```

South	West	North	East
–	–	1♣	Pass
2♦	Pass	2NT	Pass
3♣	Pass	3♦	Pass
5♦	All Pass		

South should have bid three hearts over North's
three diamonds. That would have led to the more
normal 3NT. Still, the play's the thing.

West led the seven of clubs which ran to declarer's
queen. Declarer drew trumps, played a spade to the
ace and ran the queen of spades. West won the king
and played a second club. East took two tricks in the
suit and declarer was one down. Can you do better?

What went wrong?

It is pretty clear that it is East who has the ace of clubs. In that case declarer made a 50-50 guess in the spade suit when he should have seen that it did not matter *who* had the king. He could guarantee his contract.

What should declarer have done?

Look what happens if declarer takes an ordinary spade finesse instead of the ruffing variety. If West has the king, no problem. If East has the king he wins the trick but can do no harm. In the fullness of time declarer can take three spades, two hearts, five diamonds and one club.

The play

Trick 1 : Win the queen of clubs.
Tricks 2-5 : Draw trumps, discarding a heart from dummy.
Trick 6 : Play a spade to the queen. On this occasion the queen holds.
Trick 7 : Cash the ace of spades discarding a club.
Trick 8 : Play the jack of spades discarding another club. West wins.

Trick 9: He continues with a second club to East's ten.

Trick 10: East plays the ace of clubs which you ruff.

Trick 11: Play a heart to the king.

Trick 12: Cash the ten of spades discarding a heart.

Trick 13: The last trick is your ace of hearts.

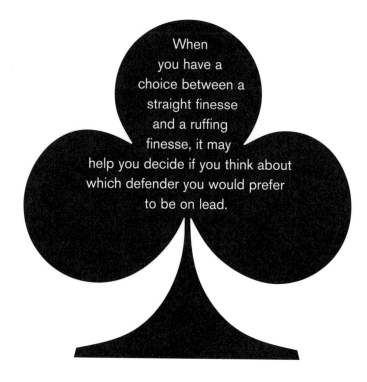

When you have a choice between a straight finesse and a ruffing finesse, it may help you decide if you think about which defender you would prefer to be on lead.

deal 15
trump control

```
           ♠ 8652
           ♥ Q7
           ♦ AQJ74
           ♣ A7
♠ KJ109    ┌─────────┐   ♠ Q
♥ A82      │    N    │   ♥ J9653
♦ 1082     │ W     E │   ♦ 63
♣ QJ5      │    S    │   ♣ K9632
           └─────────┘
           ♠ A743
           ♥ K104
           ♦ K95
           ♣ 1084
```

South	West	North	East
Pass	Pass	1 ♦	Pass
1 ♠	All Pass		

West led the queen of clubs against
one spade. Declarer won the lead
and played the ace of spades and
another spade. West thought
this an excellent turn of events
and continued to draw trumps.
Then he played clubs. In
total declarer went two
down, losing three trumps,
four clubs and a heart trick.
Can you do better?

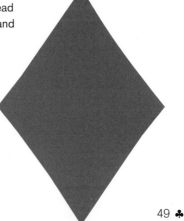

What went wrong?

Declarer lost trump control. Releasing the ace of trumps when he did was a very serious mistake. The ace of trumps is the most powerful card in the pack, whether it is held by the declarer or a defender. Choose carefully when to play it.

What should declarer have done?

Winning the club lead was fine but then he should have played a low trump from both hands. Best defence is for West to win his king and continue trumps but declarer now plays on diamonds and he is control of the hand.

The play

Trick 1: Win the ace of clubs.
Trick 2: Play the two of spades to East's queen, your three and West's king.
Trick 3: West continues with the jack of spades which you win.
Tricks 4-7: Play four rounds of diamonds, discarding, say, a heart on the fourth, which West ruffs.
Trick 8: West cashes the ten of spades.
Trick 9: West cashes the jack of clubs.
Trick 10: West plays another club which you ruff in dummy.

Trick 11: Cash the seven of diamonds discarding a heart.

Tricks 12-13: Concede a heart but make a trick with your seven of trumps, seven tricks in all.

If you have
the ace of trumps
but the rest of the suit
is rather weak it is usually
better to duck a round of the
suit before playing the ace.

deal 16
more trump control

	♠	Q82
	♥	95
	♦	9853
	♣	AJ85

♠ J109		N		♠ AK543
♥ 76	W		E	♥ A842
♦ Q1072		S		♦ J6
♣ 9732				♣ 64

	♠	76
	♥	KQJ103
	♦	AK4
	♣	KQ10

South	West	North	East
–	–	–	1♠
Double	Pass	2♣	Pass
2♥	2♠	Pass	Pass
3♣	Pass	3♥	All Pass

West led the jack of spades on which dummy played
the queen and East the king. East cashed the ace of
spades and continued the suit. Declarer ruffed,
played the king of trumps, which held, and the queen
of trumps. East won the ace and played a fourth
spade. Declarer ruffed and tried his jack of hearts,
only to find that East still had a trump. Declarer
started on clubs but East ruffed the third and cashed
a spade for one down. Can you do better?

Declarer allowed himself to be 'forced' in trumps, i.e. he 'reduced' himself to less trumps than one of the defenders (East). All would have been well if trumps had broken 3-3 but …

What should declarer have done?

Instead of ruffing East's spade at trick three he should have discarded a diamond from hand. East has no answer to this play. If he continues with a fourth spade declarer discards again from hand and ruffs with dummy's nine of trumps. Then he plays a trump and East can do no harm; if East continues at trick four with anything else, declarer simply wins and knocks out the ace of trumps before claiming ten tricks.

The play

Tricks 1-2: East wins the ace and king of spades.

Trick 3: East plays a third spade and you discard a diamond.

Trick 4: West plays a diamond which you win with your king.

Trick 5: Play a heart to dummy's nine which holds.

Trick 6: Play a second heart which East wins with the ace.

Trick 7: East returns a fourth spade which you ruff.

Tricks 8-13: Draw East's remaining trumps and the rest of your hand is high.

Note that if you were in four hearts you would have no option but to hope trumps broke 3-3. You would have to ruff the spade and try to draw trumps as quickly as possible.

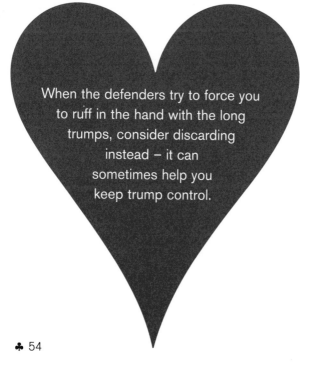

When the defenders try to force you to ruff in the hand with the long trumps, consider discarding instead – it can sometimes help you keep trump control.

deal 17
entry problems

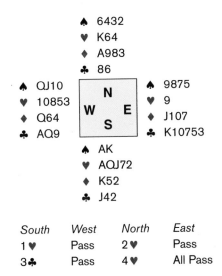

```
              ♠ 6432
              ♥ K64
              ♦ A983
              ♣ 86
♠ QJ10       ┌─────────┐      ♠ 9875
♥ 10853      │    N    │      ♥ 9
♦ Q64        │  W   E  │      ♦ J107
♣ AQ9        │    S    │      ♣ K10753
             └─────────┘
              ♠ AK
              ♥ AQJ72
              ♦ K52
              ♣ J42
```

South	West	North	East
1♥	Pass	2♥	Pass
3♣	Pass	4♥	All Pass

West found the excellent lead of a trump against
South's four hearts. This scuppered declarer's best
chance of ruffing a club in the dummy. Each time he
played clubs West would win and play trumps so by
the time dummy was void in clubs it would also be
void in trumps. Declarer saw that his only chance
was a 3-3 diamond break, so he won the trump
lead and played king, ace and another diamond. He
thought he was home when diamonds behaved but
when trumps broke 4-1 he could not reach his extra
trick and had to go down Can you do better?

What went wrong?

Declarer did well up to a point and was unlucky to find trumps 4-1. But he did not pay sufficient attention to his entry problems.

What should declarer have done?

He actually had two entries to the dummy, the king of hearts and ace of diamonds. If trumps broke badly the king of hearts would be no good, so the ace of diamonds should have been the entry he used to reach his long trick in the suit. So, draw trumps, cash the king of diamonds and duck a diamond? No, the problem with that is that a defender will win and cash three club tricks. The answer is to duck the first round of diamonds *before* touching trumps.

The play

Trick 1: Win the jack of hearts.
Trick 2: Play a low diamond from both hands. East wins with his ten.

Trick 3: East returns a spade which you win with the ace.

Tricks 4-6: Draw all West's trumps.

Trick 7: Cash the king of diamonds.

Tricks 8-9: Play a diamond to the ace and cash your long diamond, discarding a club.

Tricks 10-13: You still have the king of spades and a long trump to make, bringing your total to ten. The defenders make two clubs at the end.

The best way to keep your communications open is to duck a trick early, preserving your honors as later entries.

deal 18
lose your trump losers early

```
              ♠  652
              ♥  –
              ♦  KQJ1075
              ♣  AJ85
♠  Q                      ♠  J109
♥  AK1096      N          ♥  Q5432
♦  986       W   E        ♦  4
♣  KQ102       S          ♣  9743
              ♠  AK8743
              ♥  J87
              ♦  A32
              ♣  6
```

South	West	North	East
–	1♥	2♦	3♥
4♠	Pass	5♥	Pass
6♠	All Pass		

North/South had a good auction to the spade slam and West led the king of hearts. Declarer ruffed in dummy and cashed the ace and king of spades. When that failed to draw trumps he started on diamonds but East ruffed the second and the defenders cashed two hearts. Two down. Can you do better?

What went wrong?

Declarer again lost 'trump control'. Instead of losing the third round of trumps he should have lost the first.

What should declarer have done?

He should ruff the heart lead and duck a trump immediately. The most awkward defence is a second heart but declarer ruffs in the dummy, crosses to hand and draws trumps before cashing all his minor-suit winners.

The play

Trick 1: Ruff West's king of hearts in dummy.

Trick 2: Play a low trump from both hands. West wins with the queen.

Trick 3: West continues with a second heart which you ruff in dummy.

Trick 4: The safest way to get back to your hand is with a club ruff, so cash the ace of clubs.

Trick 5: Ruff a club to hand.

Tricks 6-7: Draw trumps.

Tricks 8-13: Cash your diamonds – twelve tricks in all.

When you can afford to lose a trump trick it is often more convenient to lose the first rather than a later one.

deal 19
loser on loser

```
              ♠ 762
              ♥ 432
              ♦ 72
              ♣ AJ854
    ♠ QJ3              ♠ 10954
    ♥ 9        N       ♥ A85
    ♦ AKQJ43  W   E    ♦ 106
    ♣ Q103     S       ♣ K962
              ♠ AK8
              ♥ KQJ1076
              ♦ 985
              ♣ 7
```

South	West	North	East
–	1♦	Pass	1♠
2♥	3♦	3♥	All Pass

West led the king followed by the ace of
diamonds against three hearts. East played
first the ten and then the six, showing a
doubleton. West continued with the
queen of diamonds.

Declarer ruffed the queen of diamonds
but East overruffed with the five and
played ace and another trump. Declarer
had to lose five tricks – one spade, two
trumps and two diamonds. Can you do better?

Declarer had eight top winners: two in spades, five in trumps and one in clubs. That left one to find and that could only come from a ruff in the dummy. Declarer should have known East would overruff the diamond because both the bidding and the play had shown he would have only a doubleton in the suit.

What should declarer have done?

If he had discarded a spade from dummy instead of ruffing the diamond he could have ruffed a spade in the dummy later.

The play

Tricks 1-2: West cashes the king and ace of diamonds.

Trick 3: West plays the queen of diamonds. Dummy and East discard spades.

Trick 4: West plays the queen of spades, say, to South's king.

Trick 5: Play the king of hearts which East wins with the ace.

Trick 6: East continues with a trump which you win.

Trick 7: Cash the ace of spades.
Trick 8: Ruff a spade in dummy.
Trick 9: Cash the ace of clubs.
Trick 10: Ruff a club in hand.
Tricks 11-13: All that are left in hand are trump winners.

If
you
think you
might be
overruffed in one suit,
try discarding instead of
ruffing and later take your
ruff in a different suit.

deal 20
preventing an overruff

```
                    ♠  QJ7
                    ♥  A64
                    ♦  KQ76
                    ♣  K62
     ♠  1085        ┌─────────┐        ♠  A
     ♥  QJ93        │    N    │        ♥  K85
     ♦  J105        │ W     E │        ♦  9832
     ♣  AJ9         │    S    │        ♣  108743
                    └─────────┘
                    ♠  K96432
                    ♥  1072
                    ♦  A4
                    ♣  Q5
```

South	West	North	East
		1♦	Pass
1♠	Pass	1NT	Pass
3♠	Pass	4♠	All Pass

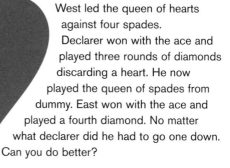

West led the queen of hearts against four spades.
Declarer won with the ace and played three rounds of diamonds discarding a heart. He now played the queen of spades from dummy. East won with the ace and played a fourth diamond. No matter what declarer did he had to go one down. Can you do better?

What went wrong?

Declarer was looking at four losers – one in spades, two in hearts and one in clubs. Clearly it was crucial for him to cash his diamonds to discard a heart before playing a trump. When that passed off peacefully with no-one ruffing he was home provided he didn't lose a second trump trick.

What should he have done?

After he had cashed his three top diamonds he should have continued with a fourth round of the suit, discarding a heart whatever East played. Now when East wins his ace of trumps he does not have a diamond to play.

The play

Trick 1: Win the ace of hearts.

Tricks 2-4: Cash three rounds of diamonds, discarding a heart.

Trick 5: Play a fourth diamond, discarding a second heart. East will win the nine.

Trick 6: Ruff East's probable heart return.

Trick 7: Play a spade to dummy's queen and East's ace.

Trick 8: Ruff East's heart return.
Tricks 9-13: Draw trumps and claim ten tricks,
merely conceding a club at the end.

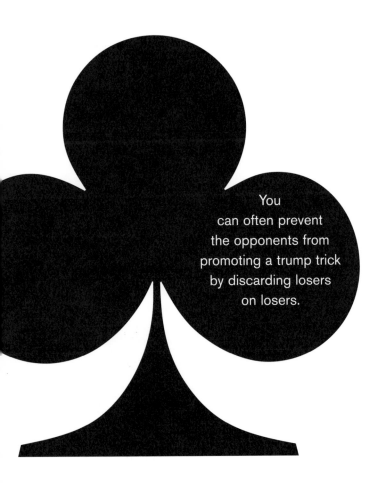

You
can often prevent
the opponents from
promoting a trump trick
by discarding losers
on losers.

deal 21
keeping the danger hand off lead

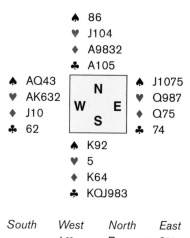

```
                    ♠ 86
                    ♥ J104
                    ♦ A9832
                    ♣ A105
   ♠ AQ43      ┌─────────┐    ♠ J1075
   ♥ AK632     │    N    │    ♥ Q987
   ♦ J10       │  W   E  │    ♦ Q75
   ♣ 62        │    S    │    ♣ 74
               └─────────┘
                    ♠ K92
                    ♥ 5
                    ♦ K64
                    ♣ KQJ983
```

South	West	North	East
–	1 ♥	Pass	2 ♥
3 ♣	3 ♥	4 ♣	All Pass

West led the ace of hearts against four clubs and continued with the king of hearts.

Declarer ruffed and drew trumps in two rounds. He then played the king, ace and another diamond, but East won and played a spade through his king and he had to go one down. Can you do better?

What went wrong?

Declarer had four possible losers – two spades, one heart and one diamond. On the other hand, he had plenty of potential tricks in diamonds. If the suit breaks 3-2 (as it will nearly 70% of the time) he can establish two long tricks in the suit on which to discard spade losers. The problem is that if East gets the lead he will surely play a spade.

What should declarer have done?

He should have refused to ruff West's king of hearts, instead discarding a diamond. Whatever West continues declarer can now establish diamonds without letting East gain the lead.

The play

Tricks 1-2: West cashes the king and ace of hearts; you discard a diamond on the second round.

Trick 3: West continues with a third heart, which you ruff.

Tricks 4-5: Cash the king and queen of trumps. In this instance that completes the drawing of trumps but even if it did not you should switch your attention to diamonds because you will need a trump entry later to reach the established suit.

Tricks 6-8: Cash the king and ace of diamonds and ruff a diamond.

Trick 9: Cross to dummy with a trump, on a different lay-out drawing the last remaining trump.

Tricks 10-11: Cash dummy's nine and eight of diamonds, discarding spades from hand.

Tricks 12-13: There is still a trump left for a tenth trick. You just lose a spade at the end.

If there is one defending hand that you would like to keep out of the lead, think about discarding your losers on his partner's winners.

deal 22
don't forget the bidding

	♠	762
	♥	10652
	♦	AQJ106
	♣	6

♠ KQJ83				♠ A9
♥ K	**N**			♥ 984
♦ K72	**W**		**E**	♦ 854
♣ KJ32		**S**		♣ 109874

	♠	1054
	♥	AQJ73
	♦	93
	♣	AQ5

South	West	North	East
–	1♠	Pass	Pass
2♥	Pass	3♥	Pass
4♥	All Pass		

West led the king of spades against four hearts.
East overtook with the ace and returned a spade to
West's jack. West cashed the queen of spades,
East discarding a club. West continued with
the two of clubs. This ran round to
declarer's queen. Declarer now cashed the
ace of clubs, ruffed a club in the dummy
and led the ten of hearts, running it when
East played low. This lost to the king and declarer
was one down. Can you do better?

What went wrong?

Declarer failed to listen to the bidding. Sure, West had already turned up with the king, queen, jack of spades and king of clubs. He needed the king of diamonds for South to succeed. That already adds up to twelve, so he did not need the king of hearts. Right? Right, but what about East? He had passed his partner's one spade opening and had already turned up with an ace. There was no room for him to have a king as well or he would have responded 1NT.

What should declarer have done?

He should have laid down the ace of hearts and dropped West's singleton king.

The play

Tricks 1-3: The defenders cash three spades.

Trick 4: West switches to the two of clubs which you win with the queen.

Trick 5: Lay down the ace of hearts. On this occasion you are lucky and West's king falls.

Tricks 6-7: Cash the queen and jack of hearts, drawing East's trumps.

Trick 8: Play the nine of diamonds, running it when West plays low. In the same way that you knew that a heart finesse could not succeed, you also know that the diamond finesse must succeed.

Tricks 9-10: Play a diamond to the queen and cash the ace of diamonds, discarding the losing club (you could equally well ruff this in the dummy).

Tricks 11-13: Claim the remainder with the ace of clubs and two master trumps.

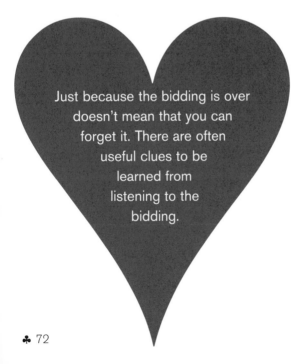

Just because the bidding is over doesn't mean that you can forget it. There are often useful clues to be learned from listening to the bidding.

deal 23
what is the distribution?

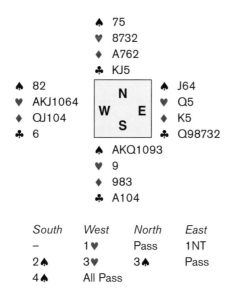

```
            ♠ 75
            ♥ 8732
            ♦ A762
            ♣ KJ5
♠ 82                         ♠ J64
♥ AKJ1064         N         ♥ Q5
♦ QJ104      W       E      ♦ K5
♣ 6              S          ♣ Q98732
            ♠ AKQ1093
            ♥ 9
            ♦ 983
            ♣ A104
```

South	West	North	East
–	1♥	Pass	1NT
2♠	3♥	3♠	Pass
4♠	All Pass		

North did well to raise to three spades. He knew that
his partner would have a good suit to come in over
1NT and that his minor-suit cards would be useful.

West led the ace of hearts followed by the king of
hearts which declarer ruffed. Declarer then drew
trumps and, expecting West to have most of the
high cards, played the ace of clubs and another
club, intending to finesse. When West showed out
he had to go one down. Can you do better?

What went wrong?

There was no great rush for declarer to take the club finesse. Declarer could afford to try diamonds first. After all, if that suit breaks 3-3 declarer doesn't need a club finesse at all. Declarer should have put off the critical decision until the last possible moment in the hope that he might find out something useful about the hand.

What should declarer have done?

Declarer should ruff the second heart and draw trumps, noting that West had a doubleton. He then ducks a diamond. When he later tries ace and another diamond and West turns up with four cards in the suit he knows that West can have only a singleton club and now the right play in that suit becomes obvious.

The play

Trick 1: West cashes the ace of hearts.
Trick 2: West continues with the king of hearts, East dropping the queen. You ruff.
Tricks 3-5: Draw trumps, noting that West started with a doubleton.

Trick 6: Play the nine of diamonds, ducking in dummy whatever happens (though you could just as easily play ace and another). This time West plays the ten of diamonds on the nine, which wins the trick.

Trick 7: West plays another heart which you ruff in hand.

Tricks 8-9: Play ace and another diamond. West wins with the jack as East shows out.

Trick 10: West plays the queen of diamonds which you ruff in hand.

Trick 11-13: You now have only clubs left in both hands but you know that West's original distribution was 2-6-4-1. So with 100% certainty you play a club to the king and then run the jack, claiming the last trick when East shows out. Ten tricks in all.

The bidding can tell you a lot about the distribution of the defenders' hands as well as about the high cards.

deal 24
a clue from the lead

```
              ♠ QJ43
              ♥ KQ10
              ♦ K1032
              ♣ 75
♠ K                          ♠ 876
♥ 762        ┌─────────┐     ♥ 94
♦ AQ5        │   N     │     ♦ J9864
♣ AQJ863     │ W   E   │     ♣ K42
             │   S     │
             └─────────┘
              ♠ A10952
              ♥ AJ853
              ♦ 7
              ♣ 109
```

South	West	North	East
–	1♣	Pass	Pass
1♠	2♣	3♠	Pass
4♠	All Pass		

Declarer bid very aggressively, liking his undisclosed five-card suit.

West led the six of hearts against four spades. Declarer won in dummy and ran the queen of spades to West's king. Given a second chance West was quick to make sure his side took its three minor-suit winners and declarer was one down. Can you do better?

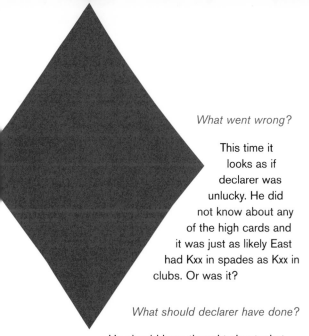

What went wrong?

This time it looks as if declarer was unlucky. He did not know about any of the high cards and it was just as likely East had Kxx in spades as Kxx in clubs. Or was it?

What should declarer have done?

He should have thought about what would have happened if East *had* had Kxx in spades instead of Kxx in clubs. True, East would not have bid or played any differently. But what about West? If you had AKQxxx in a suit wouldn't you at least try one of them at trick one? The opening lead should have told declarer that East had the king of clubs and therefore had no room for the king of spades.

The play

Trick 1: West leads the six of hearts which you win in dummy with the queen.

Trick 2: Play a spade to the ace, this time dropping West's king.

Tricks 3-4: Finish drawing East's trumps.

Tricks 5-8: Cash four heart tricks, discarding clubs from dummy.

Trick 9: Play a diamond which West wins with his ace.

Trick 10: West plays a second diamond which you win with the king, discarding a club from your hand.

Trick 11: Ruff a diamond in hand.

Tricks 12-13: Ruff a club in dummy and claim the last trick with a trump in hand. Twelve tricks in all.

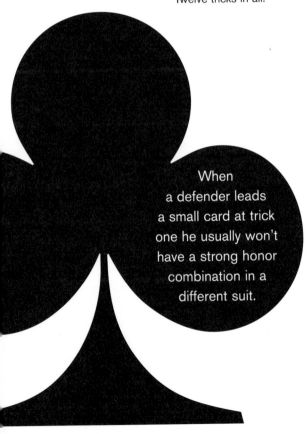

When a defender leads a small card at trick one he usually won't have a strong honor combination in a different suit.

deal 25

how many tricks do you need?

```
              ♠ K8742
              ♥ KJ104
              ♦ 9
              ♣ J109
   ♠ –                       ♠ QJ65
   ♥ 7653        N           ♥ 98
   ♦ KQ1084    W   E         ♦ 7632
   ♣ 8653        S           ♣ K74
              ♠ A1093
              ♥ AQ2
              ♦ AJ5
              ♣ AQ2
```

South	West	North	East
2NT	Pass	5♣	Pass
3♠	Pass	4NT	Pass
5♣	Pass	6♠	All Pass

West led the king of diamonds against six spades. Declarer won with the ace and laid down the ace of spades. When West showed out he had to go one down. Can you do better?

What went wrong?

There is a 100% play in the spade suit if you want to restrict your losers in the suit to one. What you must do is play the ten of spades immediately and run it if West follows. This will probably lose to East's queen or jack but on the next two rounds your ace and king will draw the remaining trumps. If West shows out on the ten of spades you rise with dummy's king and play a second spade. If East plays low, you just cover his card; if East splits his honors you win the ace. Then your nine will drive out East's other honor, while the eight in dummy will draw his remaining trump.

The trouble is that although this play restricts losers to one, it offers very little chance of no losers at all. If the suit breaks 2-2 then declarer need not lose a trump trick and would make his slam even if the club king were with West.

What should declarer have done?

He should have *started* by taking the club finesse. If it works he can then take the safety play in trumps; if it loses he has to try to avoid a trump loser.

The play

Trick 1: Win the ace of diamonds.
Trick 2: Play a heart to the ten.

Trick 3:   Play the jack of clubs. On this occasion everyone plays low. Now you can afford the safety play in trumps.

Trick 4:   Play the two of spades from dummy. East plays low and you play the nine. West shows out. Notice that the safety play in trumps can be started from either hand.

Tricks 5-6:   Cash the ace and king of spades.

Trick 7:   Play a heart to your ace.

Trick 8:   Play the queen of hearts, overtaking with dummy's king. East ruffs this trick.

Trick 9:   Ruff East's diamond return in dummy.

Trick 10:   Cash the jack of hearts discarding your queen of clubs.

Tricks 11-13:   Play a club to your ace, ruff your last diamond and at trick thirteen you have a master trump.

You sometimes have to take a finesse in a side suit to find out if you can afford a trump loser.

deal 26
simple elimination

	♠ AJ983	
	♥ AQ10	
	♦ A6	
	♣ K73	

♠ 105		♠ 2
♥ 876	**N**	♥ KJ93
♦ QJ1093	**W E**	♦ 542
♣ Q102	**S**	♣ J9865

	♠ KQ764	
	♥ 542	
	♦ K87	
	♣ A4	

South	West	North	East
1♠	Pass	4NT	Pass
5♦	Pass	5NT	Pass
6♥	Pass	6♠	All Pass

West led the queen of diamonds against six
spades. Declarer won with the ace, drew
trumps and played a heart to the ten.
East won and played a second
diamond. Declarer won with the
king and played a heart to the
queen, losing to dummy's king.
One down. Can you do better?

What went wrong?

There were no losers at all except in the heart suit. Declarer was a little unlucky to go down since, if West had either or both of the king and jack of hearts (roughly 75% of the time), he would have made his contract. But declarer could have guaranteed his contract 100% of the time.

What should declarer have done?

After he had won the diamond and drawn trumps he should have played off all his cards in the minor suits, ruffing a diamond in dummy and a club in his hand, so that all he had left in both hands were hearts and trumps. When he then plays a heart to the ten, East has no choice but to return a heart into dummy's ace-queen or give declarer a ruff and discard.

The play

Trick 1:	Win the ace of diamonds.
Tricks 2-3:	Draw trumps.
Tricks 4-5:	Play the king of diamonds and ruff a diamond.
Tricks 6-8:	Cash the ace of clubs, play a club to the king and ruff a club.

Trick 9: Play a heart to dummy's ten which East wins with the jack.

Trick 10: East has two unpleasant alternatives. He could play a heart into dummy's ace-queen, allowing you to avoid losing to his king but this time that is not what he chooses. Instead he plays a club. You discard the four of hearts from hand and ruff in the dummy. This play of a suit in which both opposing hands are void is known as a 'ruff and discard'.

Trick 11: Cash the ace of hearts.

Trick 12: Ruff a heart in your hand.

Trick 13: Claim the last trick with a trump.

Finesses are a very useful tool but the expert tries to get his opponents to take them for him.

deal 27
an extra chance

```
                ♠ 8742
                ♥ AQ75
                ♦ A6
                ♣ Q86
  ♠ QJ10      ┌─────────┐    ♠ 3
  ♥ 83        │    N    │    ♥ J1092
  ♦ K10743    │  W   E  │    ♦ J985
  ♣ 1073      │    S    │    ♣ J954
              └─────────┘
                ♠ AK965
                ♥ K64
                ♦ Q2
                ♣ AK2
```

South	West	North	East
–	–	1♣	Pass
2♠	Pass	3♠	Pass
4♣	Pass	4♦	Pass
4NT	Pass	5♥	Pass
6♠	All Pass		

West led the queen of spades against South's
excellent slam. Declarer won the king and drew a
second round of trumps. He then played three
top hearts, hoping they broke so he could
discard his diamond loser. Unfortunately
West ruffed the third round and played a
club, so declarer had to lose a trick to the king
of diamonds. Can you do better?

What went wrong?

Declarer missed his extra chance which was that of West being the one with the king of diamonds. If that was the case he was home.

What should declarer have done?

At some time West is going to make his trump trick and declarer should choose that moment carefully. He wants to force West to lead a diamond or give him a ruff and discard. Declarer should play off his top clubs before playing hearts. Then if West ruffs a heart he will not have a safe exit card. He will have to play a diamond which declarer can run round to his queen. Provided West has the king declarer will make his slam.

The play

Trick 1:	Win the king of spades.
Trick 2:	Cash the ace of spades.
Tricks 3-5:	Play three rounds of clubs.
Tricks 6-8:	Play three rounds of hearts. West discards on the third.
Trick 9:	Ruff your fourth heart. West discards again.

Trick 10: West knows perfectly well that he has nothing but diamonds, so he is in no hurry to gain the lead. By refusing to take his trump winner he has left you with a chance to go wrong. It is time to make him give you your twelfth trick, so play a trump. West wins the jack.

Tricks 11-13: West duly exits with a diamond, which you run round to your queen. You claim the last two tricks with the ace of diamonds and a trump.

Elimination play does not always make your contract certain; sometimes it merely gives you an extra chance.

deal 28
a guess becomes a sure thing

```
              ♠ KJ1064
              ♥ 86
              ♦ J42
              ♣ K103
  ♠ 97                    ♠ 8
  ♥ Q10743      N         ♥ KJ95
  ♦ AK3      W     E      ♦ 10876
  ♣ Q42         S         ♣ 9865
              ♠ AQ532
              ♥ A2
              ♦ Q95
              ♣ AJ7
```

South	West	North	East
1♠	Pass	3♠	Pass
4♠	All Pass		

West led the ace of diamonds against four
spades. He continued with the king of diamonds
and another diamond. Declarer won the
queen and drew trumps. Now, thinking
that as West had the high cards in
diamonds East was more likely to
have high cards elsewhere, declarer
played a club to the king and a club
to his jack. That lost to West's queen
and declarer also had to lose a heart. One
down. Can you do better?

What went wrong?

Declarer missed a sure fire thing here. West found an unfortunate early defence which should have left declarer in a position to claim his contract.

What should declarer have done?

After drawing trumps all he had to do was play the ace of hearts and another heart and table his cards. Whichever defender won had two unhappy alternatives. Firstly, he could play a club, finding the queen for declarer. Secondly, he could play a red suit, allowing declarer to ruff in one hand while discarding a club from the other.

The play

Tricks 1-2:	West cashes the ace and king of diamonds.
Trick 3:	Win the queen of diamonds.
Tricks 4-5:	Draw trumps.
Trick 6:	Cash the ace of hearts.
Trick 7:	Play a low heart from both hands. West wins the ten.
Trick 8:	West plays a club.
Tricks 9-13:	You claim the rest.

When a defender is thrown in in this type of
position he will usually prefer to open up a suit
rather than knowingly give you a ruff and discard.
Here it didn't matter what West did, he could
not escape.

Never
open up tricky
suit combinations
yourself if you
can force an
opponent to
do it for
you.

deal 29
much better than a finesse

```
              ♠ A4
              ♥ 107642
              ♦ K53
              ♣ A106
♠ J1092                      ♠ Q865
♥ K5         N               ♥ 8
♦ 862     W     E            ♦ QJ1097
♣ Q743       S               ♣ J82
              ♠ K73
              ♥ AQJ93
              ♦ A4
              ♣ K95
```

South	West	North	East
South	*West*	*North*	*East*
1 ♥	Pass	4 ♥	Pass
4NT	Pass	5 ♥	Pass
6 ♥	All Pass		

Exuberant bidding by South led to a reasonable slam.

West led the jack of spades against six hearts. Declarer won the ace in dummy and took the trump finesse. He later had to lose a club and that was one down. Can you do better?

What went wrong?

Declarer pinned all his hopes on the heart finesse. Once that was wrong the hand was over. He should have seen that, if he could force the defenders to open up the club suit for him, he might be able to avoid a loser in that suit.

What should declarer have done?

He should have refused the heart finesse. Sometimes when the king is singleton (about 26% of the time), he would make his contract straight away, but in addition to that he would make his contract much of the time when the king was doubleton because the player with the king of hearts would have to open up the club suit. To do that of course, he would first have to 'eliminate' spades and diamonds.

The play

Trick 1: Win the ace of spades.
Trick 2: Play a heart to the ace.
Tricks 3-4: Cash the king of spades and ruff a spade in the dummy.

Tricks 5-7: Cash the ace of diamonds, then the king of diamonds and ruff a diamond in hand.

Trick 8: Play the queen of hearts. West wins with the king.

Trick 9: West plays a small club. You play low from dummy and win East's jack with your king.

Trick 10: You now have a club finesse where there was none before. Your extra chance. Play a low club to dummy's ten.

Tricks 11-13: Cash the ace of clubs and two remaining trump tricks.

Where possible choose a line of play that offers two chances rather than put all your eggs in one basket.

deal 30
dummy reversal

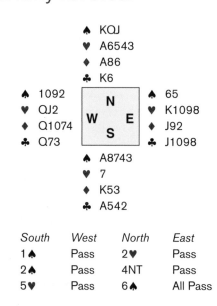

```
              ♠  KQJ
              ♥  A6543
              ♦  A86
              ♣  K6
   ♠  1092         N        ♠  65
   ♥  QJ2                    ♥  K1098
   ♦  Q1074     W     E     ♦  J92
   ♣  Q73          S        ♣  J1098
              ♠  A8743
              ♥  7
              ♦  K53
              ♣  A542
```

South	West	North	East
1♠	Pass	2♥	Pass
2♠	Pass	4NT	Pass
5♥	Pass	6♠	All Pass

North was guilty of some serious overbidding on this hand.

West led the queen of hearts and declarer surveyed dummy glumly. He won the ace, played the king and ace of clubs and ruffed a club. He came back to the king of diamonds and ruffed his last club. He hoped that a defender had been dealt ten-nine doubleton of trumps. Not this time. He had to lose a trump as well as a diamond. Can you do better?

What went wrong?

This is one of the most difficult plays in the game to spot but is quite straightforward once you have thought of it. It certainly has no place in a beginner's book, though, but I am hoping to inspire you to improve by showing you something of what is possible. Declarer's line of play was very unlikely to succeed but there is a line that has a very high chance of success. All it needs is a 3-2 trump break and a 4-3 heart break.

What should declarer have done?

Declarer has five winners outside the trump suit, six if he can establish the thirteenth heart. He was trying to generate extra trump tricks by ruffing in dummy when he should have been looking at ruffing hearts in *hand*. He can make six trump tricks in one of two ways: either by taking one ruff in dummy or by ruffing *three* times in *hand* which, together with his king-queen-jack, makes six. But by ruffing hearts in hand he will also establish a long card in that suit to bring his trick total to twelve. Follow the play overleaf.

The play

> Trick 1: Win the ace of hearts.
>
> Trick 2: Ruff a heart.
>
> Trick 3: Play a spade to dummy's jack.
>
> Trick 4: Ruff a heart.
>
> Trick 5: Play a spade to dummy's queen.
>
> Trick 6: Ruff a heart with the ace of spades.
>
> Trick 7: Cross to dummy with the king of clubs (or ace of diamonds).
>
> Trick 8: Cash the king of spades, drawing West's last trump.
>
> Tricks 9-13: Cash the long heart, ace and king of diamonds and the ace of clubs, conceding the thirteenth trick but making your slam.

This hand is really quite difficult, so do not worry if you do not understand it. Try dealing the four hands and play it out card by card.

When dummy's trumps are strong, consider ruffing losers in your own hand and drawing trumps with dummy's.